# HOOD
# VACATIONS

# HOOD VACATIONS

Michal "MJ" Jones

www.blacklawrence.com

Executive Editor: Diane Goettel
Cover Design: Crisis
Cover Art: "At the Carwash Pink" by James Bradley McCallum
Book Design: Amy Freels

Published 2023 by Black Lawrence Press.
Printed in the United States.

*For my family:*
My mother, the writer.
My Pops and two brothers, the rhythm section.
My son, the heartchild.

# Contents

*iii. comings.*

# i. goings

# Gone

*after Arisa White*

We believe we are scarce. We believe
unknowing. I wake unafraid embracing—you
have seen the silver screen fall. We fight, are
star-gazing its might, race into dusk the
arid space. Gave it my best shot at most
disgruntled shrug at least. We were mighty beautiful
once, in golden dust. I rub this love a sacred thing,
penance for our despair. I believe we are scarce, that
we sum up holes in the whole of what happened.

# At the San Pablo & 34th Ave Filling Station

Black folk scream at each other—
        off some poison we swallowed to
        bring back rainbow soap colors.

It shatters my psyche
        to a ragged rattled breath,
sets my teeth on edge,
        makes me squeeze the nozzle
        that much harder.

Pumping gas wasn't always a trigger.

On pit stops toward Philly, we kids hopped out
        to stretch our daddylong legs, got high
        off gasoline fumes, stuffed faces
        with beef jerky & pork rinds
greasing thick petroleum on our lips—

On special days we'd go through carwashes.
        Pops became a pirate
        and the huge tentacles
        scrubbing down the car's sides
        lathered Leviathans
        we raised blades to.
        And there'd be screaming.


        Tear-streaked laughter & *Lemonheads.*

            That soursweet.

# And Everything Nice

*after Wanda Coleman*

Before we warred
there was sweet.

We would sneak the stuff—
our saccharine secret—

somehow sure it made us sinners.
It started at four (or sometime before):

Slurping of Log Cabin syrup
right down from its cap,

Brother & I howling. Passed it back and
forth on Saturday mornings. We'd

rocket across grasshopper green yard
til fuel burnt up & needed

re-stocking. We sweetened unnatural
places: Brown rice n chicken,

Kraft mac n cheese,
or guzzled it straight no chaser,

let grains dissolve in
gluttonous caverns.

Stirred six cups into Kool-Aid pitchers.
Before-during-after we learned

of bitterness, of absence,
we slammed sugar unsupervised.

Knew nothing of what
too much could do to our

insatiable bodies. Knew nothing
of restraint. Knew nothing of life's

undoing. But we knew enough
to keep this secret sacred &

beneath the kitchen table.

# Rita's on Stenton

*"What you know about struggle? Bout real shit?*
*You take hood vacations, you don't stay there."*

> I am nine, caramelized in summer's time,
> cradled in our van, en route to Philly.
> Brother and I, chestnut and beige, sleep deep
> while the night sky blues to pale morning.
> We wake in Ohio, turnpike in sight,
> eager and saving our breaths for wishes.
> Up front, Pops rocks to *Heartbeat Reggae Now,*
> drums the steering wheel, thrumming hot leather,
> his rearview gaze concerts its camouflage.

*"Suburb soft, high yelluh bougie behind.*
*Haven't had to work for nothin, have you?"*

> Pops cruises through tumultuating earth,
> tunnel then green, tunnel then falling rocks,
> until hills fall flat as his promises.
> We pummel old man with *"are-we-there-yets,"*
> Pops, cool and sunglassed, trades tracks to Jilly,
> who asks if he remembers loving her.
> Silent stoic, he rolls past rowhomes.
> Ivy swallows red bricks, drapes down friezes,
> white van a golf ball against verdant shrubs.

> The car slows, our heartbeats quicken to gold.
> We do not pause for a dawdling Pops—
> we bolt, slap happy, to grammama's door.
> We jump up high, beating chests, buzzing bells,
> hot sand overflowing our thin-skin frames.
> My sweet giraffe of a cousin appears,
> I fling my arms around his bag of bones.
> I straddle-dance the archway, swivel back,
> and see Pops still there.

*"Took a beatin to get y'all what you got.*
*You understand? I'm takin a beatin."*

He folds his cinnamon hands, looks misplaced—
like a praying mantis in wooder ice—

with his back to the hood.

# 1998

It's 1998. As far as I know,
body parts grow
from bean sprouts.
I plant one deep inside myself
and hydrate it in Sunday afternoon bathwaters,
pray for extensions outside my self
to formulate. Big Bang, sprout up,
finally make me make sense.

The caterpillar I grow in
an emptied Welch's grape bottle
never leaves its chrysalis,
caught between phases.
My daddy leaves, moves out and on.
And the appendage does not grow,
stays mythical, a mystery.

And just like that—
I do not believe in magic.

# Invocation

Enough shiftless hotel lobbies and
soon chlorine becomes home.
Pops left a mammoth cave in my bedroom door
upon premature departure, flew his truck
straight through it.

Monsters from down deep—
horned winged cloaked shadowlings—
crossed the veil, cursed me an omnipotence.
The summer our distance thickened,
everything else was thin. My hollow body,
gilded air, cerulean atmosphere
splayed across vision.

Labyrinthine tongues howled their way up my
bottle mouth, no language of man.
Guttural prayers, sound alone. An unyielding grief.

When Pops rammed his steel chariot through
veins capillaries chambers & out the walls of
my heart, leaving a five-point wound, I was
nothing corporeal. Just slimmed
into stardust.

# "That and 52 cents will buy you a cup of coffee."

Coin laundry is out of the question.
No sweltering laundromats in humid season.

In the blue house on Dibble St., a plastic bumblebee basket
is overcome with divorced socks and mesh shorts.

We got our own machine down in
the concrete slab basement, next

to the sump pump where me & brother think
bodies get dumped. One birthday sleepover,

I tell Lesley there's skeletons in there,
she calls mommy, gets taken back to her house.

Coin laundry was never a concern,
coins aplenty crowd couch cushions.

We got it all right here.

I'm just a dime when mama teaches me
how to separate the darks
                              from lights,

demonstrates tri-fold creases. She's got tired
in the eyes, robed in black since her mother died.

She plays Solitaire Till Dawn til dawn,
enters Publishers Clearing House, insists,
money *can* buy you some happiness.

But—we got some money, our own machine.
Lots of coins, stacked casino chips.

Still—she got no smile.

# Mama's Weight

Made a tethered wicker boat on a charcoal lake;
she submerges slow enough to forget her origins.
A dying so long I'm unsure when to begin the wake.

Buried in riverbed muds long ago.
Hasn't energy to say a word or to
keep sleep from taking over her disembody.
That profound melancholy makes me squirm sometimes,
that density. Or I am righteous and angry—
I have stepped onto many flights
and train tracks to reach her.
Tried to stand in front of that screen in her eyes.
How could she abandon me
this way? In the way she always has, yes.

But I hold tight to her love's cradle &
remember the extra squeezes on top of her embrace,
how she dials the calls I don't want to, or can't make.

And listens better over the phone.

# In the Wake of a Transfer

*for Nia Wilson*

I.
MacArthur was not supposed
to be where your
line ended—                                    *Nia's gone*


You were to return home,
ride ricketing rails deep East,
transfer your long way Home—          *A liquified river of blood*


Graduate with honors, make
beats bend corners hold hands,
be eighteen—                                     *Cleft carotid rests under tarp*


You swallowed ancestral
fear to step onto that platform,
your sisters kept close by—               *9-car Dublin/Pleasanton in 2*
                                                              *minutes*


A scream like
that ceaseless, sparking grate
will spear a humid night—                  *She illuminates the tunnels*


And where do you journey now?
And what sense do we make of this?
Where will your mother's body breathe?     *In supernova brightness*

II.
In the morning, when Her train comes, my nails punch lunes into my palms.
In the morning, Black women gather beneath unseen umbrellas—scatter plots
along gray platform—lined against the walls. In the morning, Black women
downcast. Avert their gazes from oblivion, necks weighted with recall. I
boomerang a rage white. Slice a crescent sharp enough to sever tongues that
utter this:        *senseless. Senseless.*

*Senseless.*
when children
become ancestors.

III.
& Mama—
        I promise I'm safe on trains here.
& Mama—
        I can hear you cry-singing for me.
& Mama—
        You gonna find your way back to breathing.
& Mama—
        There's so many colors here.
& Mama—
        Colors I don't even have proper names for.
& Mama—
        We got them dancers out here, too!
& Mama—
        Everyone, everything is conductor.
& Mama—
        Our trains don't have tracks, just kinda glide like water.
& Mama—
        It's warm here, warm like light.
& Mama—
        I'm alright, mama. I'm more than alright.

## In the Mitten's Jaw

When Illinois is too far a reach for Pops, we cruise the mitten's jaw. Frankie Lymon through Frankenmuth by nighttime Notorious B.I.G. narrates Flint. Our emcee slash disc jockey keeps heads boppin & lips from flappin to more sober matters. North star in flux, Pops drives without direction. Each hotel different, charged to plastic. Debts put down will outlive him. Whatever cost to be unbound & outbound. From Lansing, we are landless. Wander on uneasy sea legs asleep with cramps, never know one town's name from the next, sleeping with content bellies & rousing early to leave & love another. We ransack & play our way through an arcade while homes dilapidate outside & lead eats its way through steel pipes.

Brother & I begin to souvenir the dead door keys.

# All Terrain Armored Transport (AT-ATs)

*after Tongo Eisen-Martin*

>              *It's actually a common misconception—*
>              *the Port of Oakland cranes did not inspire AT-ATs!*
>                            *//*

Blue BART line
hoards its screams
to power a monster city
& shit Y2K damn near
shut down the whole operation.

*—What operation?—*

>              [If a turf dancer dances the car's length
>              he is a sharp inhale.]

          Barreling
          Grating
          Sand crabbing
          Smearing a land
          too desolate even for
          galactic imagination

               *Are we here if they*
               *don't see / hear us?*
               asks the bodiless scream

>                        —We will hold a rally in support
>                        of each of your killers—
>                                 answers Walnut Creek

Shots fired when Olympic
balled fist raised skyward
for a handle to hold

[Shots fired when Olympic
balled fist *didn't* raise skyward
for a handle to hold]

                Shooter turns sideways,
                disappears with pistol smoke &
                y'all slept 2 stops past Fruitvale

Barrel
Grate
Crate
Crab
Crapshoot
       *Bang*         Jostled awake


A spider shits a graffiti web & y'all caught up in spray canisters
      A painter streaks stars & he invents The Galaxy
            A filmmaker says Oakland ain't The Galaxy—(*phew!*)

When web-open hand grips
the car door handle
steps into the sun

He becomes
an illusioned monster & hops out
to greet a firing squad.

# Praying Mantis

At twilight
amidst fireflies
I find him in
garden cabbages,
lift him gently into an open-faced K-Swiss box.
Undisturbed. I watch him stand
still in deceptive devotion.
Spike-lined
limbs fold to an
unruly God, how any
preacher's son enchants. I'm
entranced, seduced almost. Clocks
slow as his movements
glacier before heat came.
Transfixed til
lightning bugs fade
their sleep. Mama comes over
to collect me indoors, stares at my
staring, and cautions:
be careful, those can be dangerous.

# Jazz Crusaders

O, road trip tales
O, bitter trails
Boatman sails
This land-bound vessel
on jazz-jumped axles.
Bold brass bangin
trumpets sway on
through to troubled
avenues we bend.
O, road dog,
I am freeway,
you the breeze.
O, lonesome truckers
we dip bows to—
who blow horns,
or smile and don't.
(But we keep reaching).
O, vagabonds,
no time to answer
what or how we do.
We pass on by.
We pass on through.

# The Summer My Cousin Stops Playing With Me

I don't even have mounds
rising from my peaceful chest.
He'd been the Kong to my Diddy,
ebony to my ivory fumbling of *Heart & Soul* on
Grammama's forbidden piano.

The small cousins,
we laid skinny bodies under mahogany,
cheated at Monopoly,
dueled with light-sabers in the den.
Slipped & slid down plastic-covered sofas til
grammama shouted us out onto the lawn,
whispered secrets in dim blanket forts, shared glossy-eyed,
torturous goodbyes when I'd head back to the burbs…

The summer my cousin stops playing with me
I figure he's mad we don't visit more often.
Like his life is some

        spectacle for view.

    This new cold summer,
    his hug is shoulder to shoulder,
    his look of faint disgust. He lays it out clearly
    that I can't play with *them* cause *they* boys.

Didn't know I wasn't.
Didn't know it mattered.

# Safe Passage

*With his light skin, my great-grandfather evaded a lynching in Little Rock, AR.*

He who does not illuminate *monstrous*
in cover of night / smuggles his trio

of sons / passed burning poplar / passed snapped neck.
Bundled flesh freight / secluded in burlap

laid across steel truck bed / This fair passage
the weight of witness / Devoid of black-ness

He lives / suffers only death of spirit
Safe arrival to Chicago / he dreams

of hounds at his heel / His blood—betrayal.
His shade of beige / when pressed to flame / fades white.

# Golden Oreo

*for Shaun King*

*We just as oppressed*
*as the rest matta fact*
*we more oppressed*
*can't please white or black*

*always caught between*

*two worlds got made fun*
*of for being too light &*
*it was always other niggas*
*call me high yelluh golden*
*oreo mulatto*

*to the man i'm just a nigger same as you.*

*just a nigger same as you*
*& y'all act like it was better*
*in the house than field*
*but you wasn't there to know*
*nothin were you & neither was i*

*just a nigger same as you.*

*& livin where massa slept wasn't*
*no kinda blessing he'd sell us off*
*no matter how kin to him we look*
*sell his own seed so it ain't been*
*silver spoons & crystal staircases*

*for me so don't say it again, nigger—*
*Oh my fault—*

                                                     nigga.

# Palimpsest, Urban

Sidewalk sprouted more
candles bouquets foil heart balloons,
swallowed a child whole
into its undercarriage.

Its breath copper alchemy and
lead, ruptured promises,
knee's leaps over
cracked back superstitions.

On a corner you can app map
a reroute real simple.
Bend wheels round
less troubled avenues.

Ancient streets bear the same
names as new paved ones.
New paved ones leave out
eye sores, promise you gladness.

# Popular Poisons

The view from here is trash
literal trash heap backyard junkyard
bins & tin cans beneath cross legged
freeway spewing exhaust into overworked lungs
tent reams & bent beams from crash scenes discarded
goods & rusted hoods lifted exposing guts gutter rats
OG Lyft driver takes note: *"the trash problem*
*worse here than in the city!"* & a pity
he mistook people for garbage
their thirty forty fifty sixty
years of living slapped
onto a widowed sidewalk & left
I pull up on the corner the other week
to two blonde bobbin ponytails cottontailin up
the street feet tip toeing round piss & litter & I chirp
something bitter before pulling up in my driveway
climbing stairs to my stoop & here here here
where i will on a loop look &
look down     on there.

# Praying Mantis Is Remarried

If Praying Mantis gathers us in the smoke-filled
restaurant of a hotel lobby;
If the man-bug cradles
his elbows and turns down his eyes;
If the nostrils blossom and
the lips iron tight;
If he is stoic as he wind tunnels the words
to you and brother;
If his pointer keeps tap tap tapping his elbow;
If he says it;
If he says it; if he means it—

flood fast to the floor to hide your visage.
Study the carpet's paisley, its swimming
coy fish tears,
table's gum-littered underside,
rather than his spear-lined talon,
outstretched toward your body.
Squint tight with desperation
to teleport. Origami crumble into littered scraps.

Dissolve desire to witness his flesh devoured
by this new mate.

# The Question Is:

What remains living
when a city has had its membranes swept,
a forced, grudging birth to alternate reality
where Adeline is collapsed into one lane
to free up space for bikes
on their way to yoga in
Bobby Hutton Park?

> : Placenta condensed capsules
> for onlookers to swallow
> as if they had carried
> this town in their abdomens &
> nurtured its finest yolks.

//
On BART, a lump jumps into my
throat bump and clumps up
beneath the Bay,
somewhere between West Oakland
and Embarcadero. Pins & needles
> join as company,
> Ignite a flame into my shoulders
> curve a trickle down into spine.
Cacophony of wheels on rails
soundtrack this horror flick.

Packed bodies
crowd the air I reach for.

Thoughts bounce panic strewn about.
> That teenage panic realizing
> I'm on the wrong train and ...
> This tunnel,
> this Blurred and Ravenous Terrain—
reeks of smoke, steel & iron.

If the Black man BART police just shot
was packin heat,
did he deserve to die?

      (Cuz I swear a white man
      traipsed right past the turnstile
      packing heat from a Black girl's slit throat).

If Mother Earth shakes
a January dawn awake,
was she angry over the
gulps of blood? Recalling Oscar?
Releasing tension of grief?
If the white woman
hands a dollar
to the contortionist dancer,
will he be more or less
worth his weight?

# Dove

*after 'White Turtleneck' by painter Amaoka Boafa*

Before he stepped
        out the house
Before his sneaks
        smacked the sidewalk
Before he glided
        up the stairwell
Before he trombone slid
        onto a Daly City train
Before he threw a poem &
        a lyric upside a brick wall

        He knew he was somebody, damn right, he was somebody.

Before he held a blazing
        then lilac sunset in the palms of his hands
Before he both became
        and defied the night
Before before before
        his debut onto this fog city backdrop,

He rapped at his grandmother's door with soft knuckles & awaited her
welcome. He kissed her forehead & pulled the medicine vial from his
back pocket. He poured up a golden teaspoon of the brown syrup. He
titled it to her quaking lips and she drank. He wrapped arms strong
with song around her and planted one more forehead kiss.

        Before he lifted his entire weight up
                onto the BART handlebars and suspended
                        upside-down in a God-kissed levitation

        He see-sawed two little sisters clung to each arm,
        turning and turning as a sprinkler or record does,
        pirouetting as a dancer does, as their laughs & screams
        echoed throughout the house

Before he held every kick & every snare & every bass
inside his fluid ecstatic, electric shouting body

He clad himself in the full moon. He robed his body
with a lily. He wrapped himself in snow (call him icy).
He sprouted dove wings outta his feet. He became a
cloud. He danced onto tongues of white light.

Before he rounded his shoulders & two-stepped outta the house

His mama stepped behind
him, as she does,
to watch him bob down the hill
& out of view,

mouthing the
same daily
prayer:

*Return, son, return.*

# ii. channelings.

# Chambers

The taint of a haint-saint hangs
on air in the stairwell that he passed,
filigrees life lines
etched in his youngest's flesh—
       Pops' reach on conga drum's rind

Pops palms haint's stopped heart
back to work,
reaches through
that treacherous time,
spits sweats shines
til metal rims
reflect his father's resurrected eyes

        Pops props drums
        cradled in his kneecaps,
        raises ghosts to dance among us.
        People of the park—his congregants—
        arrive rhythmless, fall upon it,
        Shook shook shaking.

Pops conguero
dip-trips the flat lines,
gives us
     *pom*        *bop  bop bop*
slaps til
raw hands
raw heart
don't ache.

*Pulse pulse -*
His father's.

     *Pulse pulse—*
       His own.

# Channelings

I.
*A closed mouth don't get fed*, it's been said.
I've called seance, brought the dead
harvest repast.
Each of them passed
with secrets on their lips.
All of them eat
with the might
of an eons-worn hunger.
Of an eons-worn hunger,
with the might
All of them eat
with secrets on their lips.
Each of them passed
harvest repast.
I've called seance, brought the dead
*A closed mouth don't get fed*, it's been said.

II.
I would declare my own blood
a tainted paint sick with rot
      if it didn't pale my skin to passing
      if I could have distinguished
      whether it was my neck or my noose.
A curse to sit so closely
      to that which hunted me,
      to share something like a secret
      held until last breath.
*Do our captors capture*
      *A place on ancestors' altar?*

III.
You must go somewhere else do something else become something else
when your eyes behold a terror / You float leave your body standing there
aboveground feet forsaking themselves an unseeing still-seeing / Images of
mulch grass salt whiter greener browner until colors go nameless but color
will always and most definitely matter.

IV.
Passage to escape the
Passage you can't.
When the blue vein
collapses and you
pass into all that
Black sea of everything,
the vein collapses in
on itself as you turn
your back to the black
breathing bodies of your
making. Make them the
outer layer of your concentric
circle and front proximity when
it benefits. Deject that arsenic
of your blood—live while you
reap its benefits. Choose to keep
it light until you've erased its
traces—then what?

V.
*But of course you remember.*
*Death is no forgetting. Taste a re-memory.*
*While you breathed you made Me enemy, tucked*
*Me under armpit in tow, shoved me into*
*black widow corners to be forgotten.*

All I wanted in life, was death.
All that I ponder in death,
        is breath.

VI.
What a tangled web I am caught in before weaving.

*What is life more than a list poem?*
Counting haunted breaths on BART steps,
plucking tulips from headstones,
a rusting red bicycle on the doormat,
bougainvillea snaking down rooftop,
bluejay narrowly missing windshield,
gut splatter—praying mantis wasn't so lucky (shoulda prayed harder),
slow lick of honey off teaspoon,
the promise of pussy at some point,
a nail in my tire soap in my eye,
a smile that makes eye corners crinkle.

& which of these stick to memory?

VII.

You were right, mama, and I should have listened: They are *not* to be trusted.

And so I will avoid them at all costs!
Turn away my own blood in pints!
If I cast a third of it out, that should do,
remove my likeness from the
slinking slithering things!
Cast the bloodspell!
Spray some decrepit porting dock in Charleston vermilion!
They can have it back!

*iii. comings.*

# Turnstiles

When I came here / lifted from mother's / abdomen like soil
I had enough lives / stockpiled to know / there is nothing to
the myth / *getting it right* / no matter how / many rotations we
spin and spin / til we're sick dizzy / son & I / In centripetal orbit,
fleshy upright turnstiles / we scream a laughter / into ether like
prayer already answered / He's exhausted bones / by nautical
twilight I gaze / between crib bars / brown skin / in deepening dusk
crest & trough / his dulcet breath / Oceans tide my looking / Perfection
my sins may deface / At star-rise ceremony / in blackness / I lift him
soft swift certain / of an un-caging / in my chest. Lay him / out just
a moment for apex / of breath / hummingbird heart / thrumming
against my life line / I could weep / at my own / capacity to hurt him &
hurt him again / Be the reason / he therapies / But for now I kiss
sweet sternum / massage soft tendrils / sprung from scalp
Stare into ceaseless /                     forgiving night.

# Unnamed

The baby arrived, 6 lbs 8 oz, 19 inches long.
Born at eight months, a little premature.
Got his shots, a 7 APGAR score,
but healthy. Ready for birth announcements.

The baby died, 150 lbs, 72 inches long.
Aged nineteen years, a little premature.
Got his shots, all 22 of them ripping his flesh,
until his life's contents—
        sepia marrow,
        three pearled push-pins,
        a sandless hourglass,
        wallet-worn portrait of two daughters—
stained the sidewalk.

Supine body left to bake into the ground.
Contusions on his wrists where he was first tethered,
and on his back where the knee broke his spine,
but otherwise healthy.
No shots to the head or his tender face, so

He was casket pretty,

Ready for postcards

# ALIVE: The Simple Acronym That May Save Your Black Child's Life!

ATTENTION PARENTS OF BLACK CHILDREN:
Teach your Black child how to stay alive during interactions with law enforcement with the ALIVE acronym! Avoid needless tragedy with these simple letters:

A is for always mind your manners!
    L is for listen and comply!
        I is for in control of your emotions!
            V is for visible hands always!
                E is for explain everything!

A-L-I-V-E: Alive! Make sure your kids LIVE, with the ALIVE acronym!

*TERMS & CONDITIONS: THIS ACRONYM ONLY APPLIES TO THOSE WHO A.) DO NOT ALREADY FIND THEMSELVES TRAINED IN THE CROSSHAIRS FROM BIRTH; B.) DO NOT MAKE THE OFFICER OR SELF-APPOINTED VIGILANTE FEEL PERSONALLY THREATENED; C.) DO NOT PLAY WITH TOY GUNS, D.) DO NOT HAVE TO HUSTLE FOR THE DAY-TO-DAY TO FEED THEIR FAMILIES, AND; E.) DO NOT HAVE MENTAL ILLNESSES.*

A-L-I-V-E: Alive! Make sure your kids LIVE, with the ALIVE acronym!

//

"I want you to know
that I have a firearm
in the car,"

says
Philando Castille, as
he reaches for
license &
registration.

(Exhibit L - listen and comply)

"Be quiet, mommy,
I don't want you
to get shooted,"

sputters from a 4-
year old's mouth as she
watches Philando Castille
bleed an atlas onto his tee,
from where she sits in the
backseat. She fears her
mother will be next, and
attempts to calm her
screams:

"Be quiet, mommy,
I don't want you
to get shooted."

(Exhibit I - in control of your emotions)

Demouria Hogg is
unconscious in his car
unresponsive
when he is gunned
down by Oakland police.
The officer who shoots him claims she had
a difficult time seeing him
through the windshield.

*I couldn't see him but swear*
*I saw him enough to see*
*him move! He reached*
*for the gun!*

~~(Exhibit V - visible hands always)~~

                                    Tamir Rice, a 12-year-old child,
                              is shot within approximately 2 seconds
                              when Cleveland police pull up on him
                                          while he plays in a park.


                                    [[Couldn't get it out in time:
                                          but, for what I'm worth
                                          —the gun isn't real.]]

~~(Exhibit E - explain everything)~~

L-I-V-E. L-I-V-
L-I-

Live.
            Live.          Live.                          Deceased.
                                                          Traumatized.
            Paid administrative leave. Live.   Alive.     Deceased.
                  Alive.  Alive.          Alive. Alive.    Deceased.
Alive.               Paid administrative leave.            Deceased.
Alive.        Alive.                                       Deceased.
Alive.                          Alive.                     Deceased.
      Alive                                   Alive.       Deceased.
Paid administrative leave.      Alive.                     Deceased.


---

Acronyms do not save lives.
Our tendency to hope /
to dream / to create alternate realities
will save us every day.

I remix this parenting prefix in memory of you:

B - Believe that the ancestors will protect our babies when systems fail to

L - Love them fiercely even in a world that is not always loving towards them

A - Ascend above, transcend the white noise

C - Carry their hearts in your hand like diamonds

K - Know your worth, black baby, know your worth.

# When fam says he could never be Trayvon cuz he knows better—


A silence                    then a tomb
grows across my mouth        deadens the roof
tastes of metal smoke              hot blood chokes

          Speech knows no tongue

      He takes my silence
      as sign that he has won
      whatever argument he is trying
      to still convince his own damn self of—
      & Not of my purpled shame
      Not of a blood river behind dammed lips

Not of the catacomb
of row after row after row after row
after row after row after row after row
of dead Black children
piled between my larynx

      and my staring infant son.

# Embrace

*for Devonte Hart*

If you had been in the car with them,
you would have washed ashore, too,
Returned as bruised bones to ocean face
Collected for headlines.
A body reduced to its parts.

I could picture it—
where they buried you alone—
But I will not, Devonte, cannot invite the image
into my trained longhand, where my son
sleeps in peace.

Instead I find you
walking grounds of Sequoia groves
in warm gilded sunlight, field
and fauna your domain. Without fear amidst
these giants, standing guard.

I will meet you there between coast
and vanished, with blackberries or whatever
sweet treat your heart and belly crave. We will eat
in damp morning. There is more
than enough to eat here.

And if you ever get scared—I do mean *ever*—
I will wrap you in these arms,
hold you ear-over-heart close,
and believe your every breath.

# The cashier has a thing for Black girls

What is the thing that
this white dyke has for me
I would like to ask
but don't just no teeth grin
into my shoulder
She's eager at my stretch
of neck is kissing
me with lifeless empty
lips is kissing me
like she just knows she'll get
this *brown shuga* is
pressing into me is
having a thing for
me or the trope of mes
that she imagines
& I don't share her same
arousal—So she
suggests a film & picks
*Madea* to prove
she's hip to this thing
she got for Black girls
ones that "look aggressive"
like me—buttercream
enough to whip bitter
sweet I mean can I
blame her for knowing what
she likes she's leaving
me an awful hickey
my eyes are open
to study crown molding.
I'm not in the mood
want to go home she begs
for me to stay my
jeans ain't moist or tightening

there's a bruise on my
trachea I'd rather
stagger home in cool
Capitol Hill mists in
yawning dawn than be
this bitch's plaything.

## "I Always Wanted to Bang a Black Boi"

Another high bright stage and I'm on it.
White girl here has written me a sonnet.
Wants to wear me as a shoe, try out my
soul to season pale flesh. My skin reason
enough or kin enough to fin her tongue
across its ash. *Do I detect a hint
of grits? Dashes of cornmeal? Paprika?
Rum? What is it? What is it? What are you?*
She sees no monkeys here. They're on her back,
whip shit at my evasive slip. I dip.
Lightened to live long enough for questions.
Go where I know she's not to follow, no.

In sky void of stars. Moon eludes its bright.
She will not embrace this curtain of night.

# Compensation

That expanse between your hand & where my slung jeans meet my tender divide
may as well be a jet ride—fuel up
You want me to hoist them up / feral feeble with belief that doing so will earn
me a form of respect after a sliced millennium of naught
You thought my poetics too bassline / hard & jagged to your ear / at once too
much & not enough
*What is the landscape of my hunger?* :: What a stupid question
Esoteric bitches elated by erasure & elusive bitesounds will have me chase my
proverbial tail & assume I don't know it's attached to me
This quotidian crow I am is a comfort warm blooded / comes with ease
*What do you sacrifice in the name of niggadom?* ::

Being left dusted /
Leaning on words /
to shield a rain of bullets.

# Record of Birth

"We haven't known each other long enough."
This was your only declaration. A bloodspell.

Still. I attended every prenatal appointment
by your side like a wheeled nightstand as you moved

In and out, in and out of hospital rooms, stood guard at
the baby shower, pressed my hand over your

bass drum belly as it pulsed with kicks and our hearts
soared, urged nurses to pay you more attention,

watched 5AM amniotic fluids cascade down onto
bathroom linoleum, drove you to the delivery room,

rubbed your sciatic nerve as you cried silent
in labor pains, watched his head groundhog

In and out, in and out of you, beheld the flight
he took cocooned in your tunnel of waters, touched

his slime-covered back / cut the cord in a fell slice,
watched gloved hands lift him onto your

flustered chest, calmed him in a voice that
had spoken and sung to him for nine months

while the nurses did their various examinations,
rocked rocked him as you rested and recovered

(and pulled him from you, protective when you
fell asleep with him in your arms in the narrow cot),

wiped meconium from his new, narrow ass,
wrote him poetry. When the social worker came

asking if you wanted to add a second name
to the record of birth, you looked at him,

glanced at me. And shook your head—

# Nature Nurture

The gardener chose the Soil and
    the Soil was good.
The Soil could have done without, but
    saw their gentle way,
How they tilled Her fertile body with
    their own calloused hands.
In early Spring, they arrived with bulbs
    and seeds of all kinds
And sweetness with which to plant them.
    The gardener dug
Neatly lined pockets to fill with seed,
    singing as they sowed:
*Oh, my dear sweet Soil, how I wonder*
    *what we will grow.*
Soil swelled with new sprouts by day,
    turned bitter by nightfall.
She feared the gardener would claim Her
    sproutings for their own.
The gardener returned faithfully
    with water in tow,
Massaging Soil's scalp and plucking
    pests from newborn leaves,
All the time singing: *oh, how I wonder*
    *what we will grow.*
Soil had become weary of all the
    gardener's "wes."
They had not grown a single thing, merely
    tended to Her seeds.
She cried to the dry sky for rainfall
    and the clouds did weep.
On the final day the sower returned
    to the Soil,
She had grown a mouth with which to speak
    and swallow them whole.

By then, Her sproutings had grown up to
    the gardener's knees.
As the gardener began to sing,
    Soil folded them
Into the earth, despite their muffled screams.
    She began to sing:
*Wind finds tree, acorn finds the ground,*
    *rain hits soil*
*And we grow grow grow. Seed rain and soil—*

*need no sower.*

# Role Reversal

I wait behind a curtain.
A minor surgery major enough to put Pops under.
I mask anxieties in front of this sensitive brown boy
who is my brother young enough for son. He is often
mistaken as such. I feel blue eyes judge my teenaged body.
We wait behind a curtain.

Old man seemed calm enough heading in. As he is.
He'll probably be fine. I hug brother-son's frail frame
in reassurance. The curtain parts. Pops is loopy.
I picture cartoon stars spinning round his head.
There are tubes and wires all around him.

He objects to his youngest child's presence—
            the most sheltered of us three kids—
I blink away tears rising at deathbed's forerunner.
Months before this day, a rear-ender car crash
ripped Pops' shoulder from its bone completely.

Today they weave him back together, leave his right arm
in a sling. Mostly silent as my stepmom drives home,
uncharacteristically chipper, Pops grows stoic silent
as we pull into a neatly tucked suburban driveway.
He lingers as I prepare to guide him inside.

He leans on me in this tender trundle, sails deflated.
Feet stomp his heart's protestations. In the doorway,
this titan, this redwood of a man falls on me with his
full, dead weight, and sobs.
*My drums. My drums. I can't play my drums.*

And he weeps, and weeps.
Like a man with nothing
to live for.

# Blemish

The room has a feel
of hot swampland
with an alligator's
temperament.

Walls bear scars of
each decibel raised battle,
war crimes to cheap
paint over drywall.

I wonder how home
this will become
to you once I've
vanished with no

more a trace than
red chips on sterile
bathroom wall,
confetti rage.

I gave it character.

Shelves I installed
bereft of checkmarked
shoeboxes, walls barren
of their paintings

Dreamcatchers and
chalkboards and love notes.
Smeared, then wiped
clean from every surface.

Call it your newfound refuge
that I have failed.

# Prequel, Saturn's

Feeling this first sorrow
      A second utterance.
Autumn citronella hands on sultry air,
sets off memory tucked away in
folds of my skullscape.
I have elongated epochs since to keep it
Strongboxed, creased its tulle into
near disappearance.
When the daydreamt animal circus
miraged into opaque blocks disintegrates,
decrepit in my imagining,
I am just as
eight-year-old crestfallen.
Just as I always have been.
And here I thought myself grown.
My baby drowses here
then he is over there—the crib empties—
then he is me
When I am
Just as sleeping
beneath a Lansing windowpane
atop hallowed cracked pinewoods
beside the dog's breath that reminds me
I'm still drowning in Clapton's river of tears.
I had held this agony at a safe offing.
Just as *come back*
*come  back*
ricochets into God's breezeway.
When memory sails home, dog-eared and worn,
All I am is
wet mache
a balloon's rapid deflate before
my shape's given.
A body bereft its liquid soul.

Torn sepia guts of the *Pilgrim* cassette
left unrewound and spilled.
Alone on my bedroom floor.
Eating dust for hunger.

# What do you encounter in the void?

*after Bhanu Kapil*

I encounter breath leaned different laid sideways.
Feeble & vulnerable.
Attach lungs to houseplant tendrils, pray they propel respiration.
My chest pocked & pinned blood dots from her dart throws. Sideways-
    turned-skyward
I ignore footprints' patter across a sterile ceiling.
I have known they watch me. Accept it like this trampled heart.
Just two fortnights ago:
some common animal in me crawled across this carpet moss,
ripped the grass as if it were rooted.
Wept itself into a puddle, humbled howl—
I have become no more than this.
Now, lain sofa-fetal,
        resigned tears roll more quiet. Become still enough to evaporate.

# Skyward & Yawn

*I. Snaggies*
Butterfly berets & beads
below my scabbed knees.
Mommy rakes my curls,
a hard grief.
Calls them snaggies—
them bunches that get caught up.
Rat tail come fails, won't do.
She wields a beast with wider teeth.
Pulls the pony like it's elastic
and yanks. I choke back yelps.
She eases, smooths creases
in my neck. Today it's braids,
clean plaits. Torn, woven, tied.


*II. Ringlets*
Let me become regal now.
The most beautiful I have been.
This has been promised.
Ms. Pamela tells me *relax* with a
cool menthol lilt. Tilts my neck
to section woolen hair. Pastes
the thick magic salve which
stings like rejection.
Or a clump of hot grits
hopped from pot to cheekbone.
Peeled grapefruit in nails bit too low.
*You'll get used to it baby, that flame.*
Soon my whole crown is snow
white slick with it. I try not to
squirm scream or shudder.
Swear I hear the shit crackle.
Out the dryer, I'm all straight.

Scalp all flakes crusted blood.
Scarred marred to its root.
Usher Raymond croons through
Wall-mounted speakers.


*III. Referee Forces Black Wrestler To Cut His Locs*
before taking the mat, or he would forfeit the match.

If you were my son's referee, I'd mortar you down to fish food. Silenced
rage fever split open like Pandora's box with no hope of calming. Love only
trumps hate when you got trumping power. If you spider one centimeter of
a finger towards my dome, my son's dome, my temple, my ancestor's ladder,
my warmth, our breath, our life, our blood—Watch these locs become black
mambas. Watch you draw back a bloody nub. Watch them constrict around
your neck & squeeze the nothing from your hollow body.

But of course I speak hyperbole—What good am I to my son from prison? You
think I don't know how his mother had to smother that magma, had to twist
the neck of dish towels, had to pace linoleum and scream into her patchwork
quilts? We all have had to bite back bile knowing damn well we'd feel better to
let it spew and burn.


*IV. Inquiry*
They always think it's
innocuous—the question:
*Is that all your hair?*
Maybe it is. Innocuous.
But it's only them that ask.
I imagine my hair store bought.
Imagine that is likely what they
want to hear from such an exchange.
I stare at the inquirer and say nothing.
He floods crawfish.
The only time
These locs wasn't *mine*:
Was lover's grind and grip
on all this *mine*.

Pulling *hard*
on this *mine*
so far up inside
I surrendered the snatch,
this hair,
      all to her.


*V. In Her Hands, I'm Made*
"Babe, will you make me handsome?"
      my request glints as
lips part ways     to birth a cornball smile

Bedroom almond eyes     survey perimeter
of a frizzied dome,     She webs out
a copper hand     smooths electrified hair,

says, "you know you already handsome."

Later, cradled between softened knees.
She reaches ceremoniously into honey-lime
tubba butta, warming balm     Her fingertips
pinch the base of one loc,
Shim-shimmying     Her many-read palms
along its length.

"Take off your glasses"
I pull from my face swiftly.
crisp edges blur to vague outlines
And let eyes come closed

No need foresight
in presence of the Lord.


*VI. Pan African Festival, Mosswood Park*
Headwrap hoodoo
here holds
locs skyward & yawn

Hair buzzed tight
nurtured lawns
fluorescent cyan &
fuchsia sown in
against jetblack tapestry
Faded sides afros high
vaseline sleek edges
peaked hair tucked hedges
Queens coifed crinkled
crowned thinness
vining vertical
tree limbs bare
earth salt peppered
feathered age weathered
charcoal heather silver honey
brilliant crimson
All shimmer this
electric sliding
paragliding ocean sea into royalty.

    —And it's *all* good.

# This Poet

*after Ross Gay*

This poet,
This tall glass
of freshwater
from river's edge,

makes memory my magic
looses locked logic
into gilded dust.

Whittles me
down to a writhing rag
wrung & wrung which remains wet.

& I'm a knee-knocked
goddamned drunk juggernaut of
bunched nerve endings,

French braided fingers on neck napes,
a deep-sleep susurration at darkness
billowed into dawn that

jostles the willow's whips, gathers
glacial eyes closed like
contented curtains.

Let me be your lilted line,
a zephyrous sigh—
I'll make it wine.

# Touch Me Not

I promise to the order of things that I will not be touched fucked or filled
before I fill fuck or touch. Your gaze disrupts. Marina breeze licks then bites.
Venus and half lune moon moan against copper aubergine //

> In your room book spines rise from the ground up & you've hung
> blank canvases. I allow [read: beg] you to strip me for painting. The
> well flows over. You spiral me into arabesque—my limbs twisted lunar
> beams. I rise to your motion //

Chest cracks heaves when you retreat from me. I weep winds / pull you back
inside / feel my order of things decompose in these miniature deaths you petal.

# Incise

*I.*
Glimmers of a ghost girl in dark water.
　　　Rose across yellow cheeks—
and blush to hide tear streaks.

Purple eyeshadow heavy enough
　　　to resemble black eye ass whoopin.
This heavy-handed seasoning its own drag.

I spoke to her torment to find rest,
　　　go forth from this place, wash her tender face.
And watched her ripple gone.


*II.*
My lover lusts
for this part of me
I have imagined
　　　　rippled away.

I am a waste
basket of becoming,
Wreckaged and crooked
daydreams.

Our fucking is seance
for flesh long grave-
site to me, resurrection
to pull me back
into hollowed conch.

Each new dalliance
who looks at me
sees a ghost girl headstone.

Could they see me &
moisten if I arrive
battle scarred?

# Three Hearts

Retreat to waters where it's okay to be a pretty nigga.
Ceremonial: hit God's Gift and let the smoke meld with rising steam,
decide between oos Anthony and 90s Mariah (Mariah wins),
piss baby oil into tub and watch lava lamp bubbles coagulate,
dash of rosemary for good measure. Bow low slow, gripping
basin edges in a squat, feel eyelids droop closed and sing-song voice
cascade off of tiles laden with condensation, sway unashamed
to love ballads. Press thumbs into soles of scaly feet, pumice the
flakes, massage suction cups in crooks of limbs, wash skunk from
the arm's trenches, sink lower, kitchen on cool porcelain,
licorice locs    float like tentacles. Crack a clandestine grin, take
pleasure as the strangest creature in the sea, born of 3 hearts.
Rinse & repeat, rinse & retreat to the cave.

# Pandemic Ode: A Partial Prayer

*after Airea D. Matthews*

Praise be to solitude silence.
Praise be to steam's ascent through grate's clenched teeth, to
outstretched knees that hop over.
Praise be to corner store bodegas stocking single roll toilet paper.
Praise be to pure lungs.
Praise be to love & its discovery under overturned & broken stone.
Praise the butterfly wings &
       whistled winds which carry them. Praise be to my son's curl pattern
       & nap [3 hours down].
Praise be to the loctician-turned-therapist
disintegrating worry with strong hands at scalp; praise be to the scalp & kitchen
the thick of it pulled in lover's grip.
       Praise be to sidewalk graffiti sprawl: LOVE IS MONEY.
Praise be to fixed mortgages & rent control.
Praise be to bob & weave wheelie poppin scraper bikes blessing Lake Merritt
with bronze & tin sunrays.
Praise the 5 paper white pelicans in synchronized syncopated swim;
       Amen to their squad goals.
Praise be to the 18 bus &
to Green Naked Ladies' blurring route's landscape.

Praise be to the awning—
       its voluptuous curvature;
Praise the teeth grazing teat, scrape scream & shout Lord's name in vain,
Praise the tight tunnel collapse around fingers.
Praise be to the sideshow
       & skid marks tires burn & singe;
       Praise be to Oakland's breathing ghosts. Praise be to
Sinaloa; to the white Goldilocks standing with no shoes on
in its parking lot; praise the shit talk & cut up within earshot.
Praise be to poets who know it & poets who don't.
Praise be to ugly ducklings who stay that way & bless.
Praise be to threaded brows; fluorescent hair; sundresses & golden wing ear cuffs.

Praise be to guitars & bodies
        after their shape, supple for strum.
Praise be to skunk
seeping outta every low parked car on this block.
Praise be to the tents sandbagging the city streets;
to stakes that hold them down; to the masked
unwavering handing out hygiene & nutrition.

Praise be to black trans praise dancers; to electrified
prayer hands.
Praise the cities of refuge.
Praise this sea of black & brown worshippers whirring still air into sandstorm.
Praise be to the uncontrolled organist; to peach cobbler;
        to jumpin shoutin cryin. Praise be to the shimmering wave of fans
        preparing for flight.
Praise be to unnamed spirit. Praise be to
        altar; to those not here; to the exiled.
Praise the leaps & weeps of faith; the rocking in arms' cradle & holler.
Praise be to tilled soil;
        to grape vines; to jasmine. Praise be to indigoes & violets;
        to the color purple.
Praise be to our skin & its basement organs; to belly's wax & wane.
Praise be to the elemental.
Praise the body & its stardust; the tear's cleansing saltwater.
Praise be to remembrance &
        to release when memory grows too heavy.
Praise be to Harvest moon bathwaters; to balm of a mother's sweet song.
Praise be to incantation, to utterance.
Praise be to the elemental.
Praise be to diaspora; to
        calloused hands & hearts thumping on in defiance.
Praise be to defiance. Praise be to hummingbird's flight.

# Acknowledgements

I extend my gratitude to the editors of publications where these poems first appeared, many in earlier versions:

'Pandemic Ode: A Partial Prayer,' *Alternative Field & Avenue 50 Studio, In Isolation Anthology*

'In the Wake of a Transfer,' *Anomaly*

'Rita's On Stenton,' *Borderlands Texas Poetry Review*

'Unnamed,' *Foglifter Journal & Press*

'This poet,' *goodbaad poetry journal*

'Embrace,' *Ghost City Review*

'Gone,' *Kissing Dynamite*

'The cashier has a thing for Black girls,' *Levee Magazine*

'Safe Passage,' and 'Palimpsest, Urban,' *Midway Journal*

'Touch Me Not,' *The Night Heron Barks*

'Record of Birth' and 'Nature Nurture,' *Raising Mothers*

'I Always Wanted to Bang a Black Boi,' *RHINO Poetry*

'Turnstiles,' *Rigorous Mag*

'Invocation,' 'Prequel, Saturn's,' and 'Praying Mantis Is Remarried,' *Small Press Traffic*

'When he says he could never be Trayvon cuz he knows better—' and 'What do you encounter in the void?,' *Subnivean*

'And Everything Nice,' *wildness*

**Deep gratitude to the following individuals and communities who have inspired, encouraged, and shaped the formation my writing, and this book:** Arisa White, Raina León, Elmaz Abinader, Tongo Eisen-Martin, Hanif Abdurraqib, Truong Tran, Juliana Spahr, Jade Cho, Jessie Ewing, Mihee Kim, Nefertiti Asanti, Darius Simpson, Mimi Tempestt, N/A Oparah, Xan Phillips, Airea D. Matthews, Patricia Smith, Aria Aber, Patricia Powell, Jason Bayani, Kevin Latimer, Miah Jeffra, Luiza Flynn-Goodlett, and countless others.

Special love to my cohorts: Lambda Literary (2022), Hurston/Wright Foundation Writers Week (2019), VONA/Voices (2018), the SF Writers Grotto, the staff of Foglifter Journal & Press, and to the students, staff & faculty of the Mills College MFA in Creative Writing program.

And to Chantel Ligget, my soft armor.